WORLD COMMODITIES
Wheat

GARRY CHAPMAN » GARY HODGES

A⁺

This edition first published in 2011 in the United States of America by Smart Apple Media.

Smart Apple Media
P.O. Box 3263
Mankato, MN, 56002

First published in 2010 by
MACMILLAN EDUCATION AUSTRALIA PTY LTD
15–19 Claremont Street, South Yarra 3141

Visit our web site at www.macmillan.com.au or go directly to www.macmillanlibrary.com.au

Associated companies and representatives throughout the world.

Copyright © Garry Chapman and Gary Hodges 2010

Library of Congress Cataloging-in-Publication Data

Chapman, Garry.
  Wheat / Garry Chapman and Gary Hodges.
    p. cm. — (World commodities)
  Includes index.
  ISBN 978-1-59920-588-5 (library binding)
  1. Wheat trade—Juvenile literature. 2. Wheat—Juvenile literature. I. Hodges, Gary. II. Title.
  HD9049.W4C455 2011
  338.1'7311—dc22
                          2010007310

Publisher: Carmel Heron   Designer: Ivan Finnegan (cover and text)
Commissioning Editor: Niki Horin   Page Layout: Ivan Finnegan
Managing Editor: Vanessa Lanaway   Photo Researcher: Lesya Bryndzia (management: Debbie Gallagher)
Editor: Laura Jeanne Gobal   Illustrators: Andy Craig and Nives Porcellato, 15; Alan Laver, 17
Proofreader: Kirstie Innes-Will   Production Controller: Vanessa Johnson

Manufactured in the United States of America by Corporate Graphics, Minnesota.
052010

Acknowledgments

The author and the publisher are grateful to the following for permission to reproduce copyright material:

Front cover photograph of wheat: 123RF/varuka

AAP/Sakis Mitrolidis, **19**; The Art Archive/Bardo Zuseum Tunis/Gianni Dagli Orti, **8** (right); Ivan Ortiz-Monasterio, CIMMYT, **29**; Corbis/Design Pics/Kelly Redinger, **12** (bottom), /Arvind Garg, **24**, /Roger Garwood & Trish Ainslie, **7**, /Ed Kashi, **14**, /Dan Lamont, **20**; CSIRO/Willem van Aken, **22**; Getty Images/AFP, **18**, /AFP/Rizwan Tabassum, **13** (bottom), /DEA/G. Dagli Orti, **8** (left), /Dorling Kindersley, **4** (iron ore), /Roger Viollet/Francoise De Mulder, **23**, /SPL/Adam Gault, **28**; iStockphoto/Selahattin Bayram, **11** (middle), /Fertnig, **12** (middle), /FotografiaBasica, **13** (top), /Grafissimo, **12** (top), /Irina Tischenko, **5**; Photolibrary/Stefan Auth, **21**, /Diaphor La Phototheque, **27**, /North Wind Pictures, **9** (bottom), /Novastock Novastock, **6**, /The Print Collector, **9** (top), /SPL/Adam Hart-Davis, **25**, /US Department of Agriculture/Yue Jin, **26**; Shutterstock/Forest Badger, **4** (oil), /Beata Becla, **10**, /dcwcreations, **11** (top), /IDAL, **4** (wheat), /ronfromyork, **11** (bottom), /Worldpics, **4** (coal), /yykkaa, **4** (sugar), /Magdalena Zurawska, **4** (coffee).

Please note: At the time of printing, the Internet addresses appearing in this book were correct. Owing to the dynamic nature of the Internet, however, we cannot guarantee that all of these addresses will remain correct.

This series is for my father, Ron Chapman, with gratitude. – Garry Chapman
This series is dedicated to the memory of Jean and Alex Ross, as well as my immediate family of Sue, Hannah and Jessica,
my parents, Jim and Val, and my brother Leigh. – Gary Hodges

Contents

Glossary Words

When a word is printed in **bold**, you can look up its meaning in the Glossary on page 31.

What Is a World Commodity?

A commodity is any product for which someone is willing to pay money. A world commodity is a product that is traded across the world.

The World's Most Widely Traded Commodities

Many of the world's most widely traded commodities are **agricultural** products, such as coffee, sugar, and wheat, or **natural resources**, such as coal, iron ore, and oil. These commodities are produced in large amounts by people around the world.

Coal, coffee, iron ore, oil, sugar, and wheat are important commodities traded around the world.

Commodities and the World's Economy

Whenever the world's **demand** for a commodity increases or decreases, the price of this commodity goes up or down by the same amount everywhere. Prices usually vary from day to day. The daily trade in world commodities plays a key role in the state of the world's **economy**.

MORE ABOUT...
The Quality of Commodities

When people, businesses, or countries buy a commodity, they assume that its quality will be consistent. Oil is an example of a commodity. When people trade in oil, all barrels of oil are considered to be of the same quality regardless of where they come from.

Wheat Is a Commodity

Wheat is an agricultural commodity. It is a type of grass that is grown as a grain crop, just like rice and barley, which are also grasses.

Why Is Wheat Important?

Grain crops provide us with more food than any other source on Earth. Wheat is used to make flour, which we use to make bread, cakes, pasta, and cookies. It is also found in many breakfast cereals. Wheat provides much of the daily nutrition our bodies need, including fiber, protein, carbohydrates, vitamins, and iron.

Wheat is used to make bread, which is a staple food in many countries.

A Valuable Commodity

Wheat's importance as a food source means it will always be a valuable commodity. Many countries produce wheat for both **domestic** consumption and for **export**.

COMMODITY FACT!

Wheat is measured in bushels. One bushel of wheat can **yield** about 42 loaves of bread! This unit of measurement was first used in medieval times.

Where Is Wheat Grown and Where Is It Consumed?

Wheat is the world's most widely grown grain crop. There are hundreds of types of wheat, grown in different regions, climates, soils, and seasons.

China

China is the world's largest wheat producer. Although its annual, average wheat harvest is about 100 million tons (91 million t), it is still not enough to feed China's massive population of more than 1.3 billion people. To make up for the shortfall, China **imports** more than 4.4 million tons (4 million t) of wheat each year.

India

India is the world's second-largest producer of wheat. Like China, India does not produce enough wheat to adequately feed its own population of more than 1 billion and must rely on imports.

A large portion of the world's wheat is grown in huge wheat fields in China.

THE WORLD'S MAJOR PRODUCERS OF WHEAT (2008)

Country	Share of Global Production (Percentage)
China	15.4%
India	11.5%
United States	9.1%
Russia	7.3%
France	5.9%

Major Consumers of Wheat

China and India, the world's top producers of wheat, are also the world's top consumers of wheat. Russia and the United States are also major consumers of wheat. These countries not only have large populations to feed, but also have staple diets that include many common wheat products, such as noodles in China, chapatis in India, bliny in Russia, and pizza in the United States.

Wheat is loaded onto a ship at Kwinana, Western Australia, for export.

Wheat as Food for Livestock

In addition to using wheat for human consumption, which accounts for more than 70 percent of global wheat consumption, wheat is also used as food for livestock. This type of wheat is called feed wheat. The major consumers of feed wheat are the **European Union** and Russia, which account for 70 percent of global feed-wheat consumption.

COMMODITY FACT!

Bread is such an essential food that ancient Egyptian governments controlled its production and distribution in order to control the population.

Timeline: **The History of Wheat**

More than 12,000 years ago in the Middle East, humans discovered that the small grains that grew on the tips of wild grasses could be ground into flour between two stones.

10,000 B.C.
In the Middle East, humans grind the small grains from wild grasses into flour, which is mixed with water to form a paste and cooked to make flat bread.

about 400
Baked goods made from wheat flour are eaten by the Greeks. They make different types of bread, cakes, cookies, and pastries.

about 500
Growing wheat is a common agricultural practice around the world. Different forms of baked goods gain popularity in different regions.

10,000 B.C.

A.D. 1
Baking is so important that the Romans build mills just to grind the grain to make flour. They also bring the art of baking to the lands they conquer.

about 1600
Wheat mills are driven by wind and water. Pastry chefs bake and sell their goods from handcarts in European streets.

about 3000
Flat bread is a staple food for many early civilizations, including the Sumerians and the Egyptians.

about 50
Baking flourishes in the Roman Empire. The Romans bake pasta, pastries, and pizza in stone ovens.

This painting of a wheat harvest was found in the Tomb of Sennedjem, Egypt.

about 7000
In Mesopotamia (an area in and around present-day Iraq), farmers grow wheat. They clear land and plant the seeds from wild grasses.

This Roman mosaic is of the goddess Ceres, harvesting wheat.

In the 1600s, windmills used the power of the wind to grind wheat into flour.

1788
Wheat is introduced to Australia by the first European settlers.

1961
The Chorleywood Bread Process reduces the time needed to bake a loaf of bread. The process is now widely used where bread is mass produced.

1928
Otto Frederick Rohwedder invents a machine that both slices and wraps bread. Sliced bread becomes popular. Wheat is the staple food for half of the world's population.

1990s
New techniques allow bakeries to mix and bake bread in under three hours. Bread making at home becomes popular.

1996
The first genetically modified wheat variety is developed in order to increase crop yields and resist diseases and pests.

A.D. 2010

1950s
Farmers plant and harvest wheat by machine. White bread is the preferred bread of the middle classes, while the poor eat whole grain bread.

1980s
Whole grain bread gains preference over white bread because of its higher nutritional value.

2010
Modern combine harvesters harvest the crop, strip the kernels from the stalks, and dump the straw in a single pass of the wheat field.

about 1800
Baked goods are delivered to homes, greatly increasing demand. Fine baked goods are served at cafés and teahouses. Grain mills are driven by steam and horses.

This drawing depicts workers baking bread in ancient Rome.

How Is Wheat Grown?

Wheat can be found all over the world because it grows well in both warm and cool climates and produces a very good yield for every acre planted.

Different Wheat Varieties

There are many varieties of wheat. Scientists develop these varieties by carefully selecting seeds from a single plant, which displays desirable properties, such as resistance to disease or a higher grain yield. **Hybrid** varieties of wheat are developed by introducing **pollen** from one plant to another plant in order to create a new variety with the best features of its parents.

Spring and Winter Wheat

Two types of commonly grown wheat are spring wheat and winter wheat. Spring wheat is planted in the spring. It sprouts soon after planting and grows quickly. By the fall, it is ready for harvesting. Winter wheat is planted in the fall. It grows very slowly through the winter, then rapidly in the spring. It is ready for harvesting early in the summer.

Hard and Soft Wheat

Hard varieties of wheat have a high protein content and are usually preferred for baking bread. Soft varieties of wheat have a lower protein content and are used to make cakes, pastries, and noodles.

Different wheat varieties have different properties. This means they are suited to different purposes.

MORE ABOUT...
Growing Wheat

Wheat can only grow in commercial amounts where the soil is fertile, and the rainfall is dependable. It is also an advantage if the land is flat, so vehicles known as combine harvesters can operate. Regions where wheat is grown are often called wheat belts.

Farming Wheat

Wheat seeds, or kernels, are planted in rows in large, flat fields. They **germinate** and grow into tall, grass-like stalks. The wheat grains we eat are at the top of these stalks.

Planting

The soil is fertilized to ensure a healthy, disease-free environment for the wheat seeds. Advanced machinery allows farmers to cut a narrow trench to the correct depth in the soil, drop the kernels at evenly spaced intervals, cover them with loose soil, and apply fertilizer in a single operation.

Germination and Growth

Soon after planting, the kernel begins to germinate. Roots form and a small shoot appears. It grows until a tiny seedling breaks the surface of the soil. The seedling then passes through several stages of growth.

Maturity

Stems, called tillers, branch out from the main shoot of the growing seedling, and groups of flowers, called spikes, develop at the top of each tiller. The spikes **mature** to form wheat heads, each bearing between 50 and 75 individual kernels. The kernels continue to grow for about a month. The wheat heads change color from green to golden as the plant reaches maturity.

COMMODITY FACT!

The kernel is the seed from which wheat grows. It has three main parts. The endosperm is the largest part, containing most of the protein. The other parts are the bran and the germ.

Preparing Wheat for Consumption

Once mature, the wheat is ready for harvesting. It is then sent to a mill, where it is transformed into a range of food products.

Harvesting

The wheat must be dry before it can be harvested. The combine harvester is used to reap (cut) the stalks; thresh (separate) the kernels from the stalks; load the kernels into a large grain cart; and eject the remaining straw into the field in a single motion.

Storage

Trucks transport the grain carts to grain elevators for temporary storage. Grain elevators are usually several stories high. A grain elevator lifts the kernels to a distributor at the top of the structure. From there, the kernels flow into large bins, or silos, where they are safely stored in dry conditions.

Transportation to the Mill

When the kernels are ready to be transported to a mill for processing, they flow once more from the bottom of the storage bins into waiting trucks or railroad cars.

Reconstitution

After the different parts of the kernel are separated and ground, they are often reconstituted, or blended together, once more. This process is used to create different types of flour.

Milling

At the mill, the kernels are ground into flour. Metal rollers separate the endosperm from the bran and the germ. The rollers grind the endosperm into fine particles to make white flour. The flour is then stored in bags.

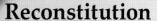

MORE ABOUT...
What Is in Wheat

There is a protein in wheat called gluten. People with celiac disease are unable to eat foods containing gluten. Gluten can make them very ill. They manage their condition by eating gluten-free foods.

13

The Wheat Trade

Wheat is an agricultural commodity that is heavily traded because many staple foods are made from it. The wheat trade is particularly important in countries with large populations to feed.

A Thriving Trade

Not all countries grow wheat or grow enough wheat to feed their populations. Brazil and Indonesia, for example, have to import large amounts of wheat, because their climates are not suited to growing it, and they cannot grow enough of it. Saudi Arabia and other parts of the Middle East import large amounts of wheat because these areas do not have enough water for farming. Additionally, not enough wheat can be grown to satisfy demand. These conditions, which occur in many countries, means the wheat trade is thriving.

Syria, in the Middle East, now imports wheat because water shortages have reduced its wheat yields.

Obstacles to Wheat Trading

There are obstacles that can make it difficult for wheat producers to sell their product in the world market. These obstacles include:
- taxes imposed on imported wheat by governments to protect the interests of domestic producers
- **subsidies** paid by governments to assist domestic producers
- **quotas** on the amount of wheat that can be imported
- high transportation costs
- **stockpiling** of wheat by importers

Exchanges

An exchange is a place where commodities, such as wheat, are bought and sold. At an exchange, wheat is bought and sold in both the futures market and spot market.

The Futures Market

Trading in the futures market involves buying and selling contracts that are set in the future. Buyers and sellers agree on a price, which will be paid when the wheat is delivered at a date in the future.

1 A wheat seller in the United States locates a buyer for a wheat futures contract in Egypt.

2 A futures contract is drawn up for the wheat to be sold at an agreed price and delivered in two months.

3 In two months, the wheat is paid for and shipped to the buyer.

The futures trading of wheat takes place in three main stages. The wheat buyer is agreeing to buy wheat at a future date for a set price.

The Spot Market

In the spot market, buyers and sellers agree on a price for the immediate exchange of goods. This means wheat is delivered to the buyer as soon as it is purchased. Once the price is paid, the wheat is transported from the granary to the place where it will be used.

1 A wheat buyer in Egypt buys wheat from a seller in the United States.

2 Cash is exchanged electronically from the buyer to the seller.

3 The wheat is immediately shipped to Egypt.

The spot trading of wheat takes place in three main stages. It is a simple transaction between a wheat seller and a wheat buyer.

Supply and Demand

The wheat trade is determined by **supply** and demand. When consumers are eager to buy the commodity, the demand for wheat increases. Consumers rely on producers to supply it.

Factors Affecting Supply

The supply of agricultural commodities is greatly affected by climate conditions. Long periods of drought, for example, can mean lower yields. This affects wheat exports. Wheat supplies can also depend on the economic focus of governments. When governments invest in agriculture, for example, the domestic wheat industry may benefit, and yields may increase. Subsidies can also affect supply. If subsidies are paid, growers may be able to farm more wheat, leading to a **surplus** that can be sold on the world market.

Factors Affecting Demand

Changes in demand for agricultural commodities tend to happen over a long period of time. This is because the main factors affecting the demand for such commodities are changes in population and income. Growing populations need more wheat for food, while income changes affect how much of a wheat-based product people will buy.

THE WORLD'S TOP EXPORTERS AND IMPORTERS OF WHEAT (2008–2009)

Exporter	Amount of Wheat Exported	Importer	Amount of Wheat Imported
United States	26,642 tons (24,220 t)	Egypt	9,482 tons (8,620 t)
Russia	18,480 tons (16,800 t)	Iran	8,481 tons (7,710 t)
Canada	17,710 tons (16,100 t)	Brazil	6,490 tons (5,900 t)
Australia	13,475 tons (12,250 t)	Algeria	5,588 tons (5,080 t)
Ukraine	12,474 tons (11,340 t)	Japan	5,500 tons (5,000 t)

Price Variations

When the global demand for wheat is greater than its supply, the price of wheat increases. In the same way, when the supply of wheat is greater than the demand for it, the world wheat-price falls.

THE RISE AND FALL OF THE WORLD PRICE OF WHEAT

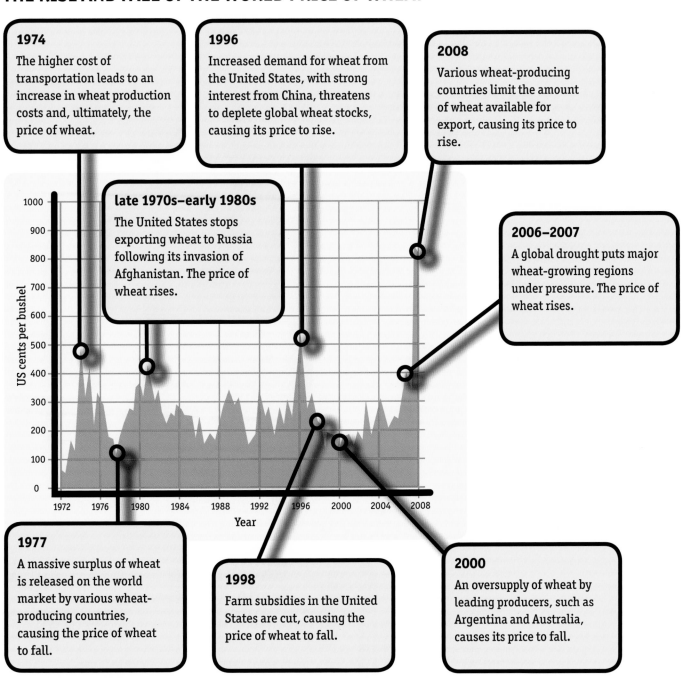

1974
The higher cost of transportation leads to an increase in wheat production costs and, ultimately, the price of wheat.

1996
Increased demand for wheat from the United States, with strong interest from China, threatens to deplete global wheat stocks, causing its price to rise.

2008
Various wheat-producing countries limit the amount of wheat available for export, causing its price to rise.

late 1970s–early 1980s
The United States stops exporting wheat to Russia following its invasion of Afghanistan. The price of wheat rises.

2006–2007
A global drought puts major wheat-growing regions under pressure. The price of wheat rises.

1977
A massive surplus of wheat is released on the world market by various wheat-producing countries, causing the price of wheat to fall.

1998
Farm subsidies in the United States are cut, causing the price of wheat to fall.

2000
An oversupply of wheat by leading producers, such as Argentina and Australia, causes its price to fall.

The world price of wheat experiences highs and lows over time. Events around the world influence the supply of and demand for the commodity, which changes the price.

Codes of Practice

Codes of practice govern the way most commodities are traded internationally. The purpose of these codes is to ensure that commodities are fairly priced and traded. The rules that govern the wheat trade are determined by the World Trade Organization (WTO) and the International Grains Council (IGC).

World Trade Organization

The wheat trade is regulated by the WTO. It is an international body with more than 150 member countries. The role of the WTO in the wheat trade is to act on complaints by trading countries and monitor the flow of wheat between buyers and sellers. The WTO aims for all wheat trades to be conducted in a consistent manner.

Resolving Disputes

From time to time, countries register complaints with the WTO about the trading practices of other countries. In 2003, the United States accused the Canadian Wheat Board (CWB) of not complying with guidelines set by the WTO. Millers and pasta makers in the United States raised the issue of gaining access to high-quality Canadian wheat. An investigation found that the CWB's import and export practices did follow WTO guidelines.

The WTO helps countries distribute food aid as part of trade agreements.

MORE ABOUT...
Trade Agreements

It is important that organizations such as the WTO help countries reach trade agreements, because in the past, some trade disputes have led to wars. Trade agreements negotiated by the WTO are usually signed by the trading countries of the world.

International Grains Council

The IGC was established in 1995 to help expand and promote trade in edible grains, including wheat. It places an emphasis on fair deals for growers, stable grain markets, and global food security. The IGC has a membership of 14 countries on its executive committee, including 6 exporters and 8 importers. It produces a monthly grain report that helps wheat buyers and sellers predict global supply-and-demand trends.

Wheat Agreements Under the IGC

The IGC was responsible for establishing a series of wheat agreements that promoted the production of wheat through improved agricultural practices. The agreements helped limit any rises in the price of wheat. In recent years, the ability of the IGC to establish wheat agreements has been diminished because some countries have moved their wheat-trading practices away from the control of a central authority.

When growers are unhappy with the price of wheat, they may resort to strikes or protests. Greek farmers protested in 2010 by blocking the roads with their tractors. The IGC emphasises fair deals for growers so that such situations can be avoided.

International Politics and Wheat

Wheat is so important in the making of basic foods globally that its production and sale are sometimes highly protected by governments. This can cause problems in the world market.

Government Subsidies

Subsidies are monetary contributions given to wheat growers by governments to help them reduce their business costs. Subsidies help protect domestic wheat industries but can have a negative impact on wheat growers in other countries. They can also have an impact on the price and supply of wheat.

Even though American wheat growers receive subsidies, the cost of farming wheat is still high. This combine harvester is used for only three weeks each year, yet costs around US$500,000.

Surpluses and Low Prices

When governments offer wheat growers subsidies, the growers tend to produce more wheat than is necessary. This is because the more wheat they grow, the more they receive in subsidies. The surplus wheat is often dumped on the world market at a very low price. For example, wheat exported from the European Union has, in the past, been sold at a price that is 40 to 60 percent below what it costs to grow.

The International Impact of Surpluses

Countries with wheat surpluses may sell their surpluses at a low price. However, by doing so, they may create difficulties for wheat growers in other countries. These wheat growers may not receive government subsidies and cannot afford to sell their wheat at the same low price being charged by their competitors. This may lead to political and economic pressure being placed on their governments to also provide subsidies. Some governments choose not to sell surpluses but to stockpile them instead. This, too, may have an international impact.

Wheat in India

Early in 2007, the Indian government banned all exports of wheat and started stockpiling surpluses. It was estimated that by early 2010, India's stockpile would reach double the amount needed in an emergency, such as a failed wheat harvest. To reduce the stockpile, India started exporting wheat again in March 2010. It is believed that by resuming wheat exports, which means an increase in supply, the world price of the commodity will start to fall.

These wheat growers in Myanmar, Southeast Asia, still harvest their wheat crops by hand. They cannot afford a combine harvester as they may not receive government subsidies or their subsidies may be too low.

Environmental Issues and Wheat

Wheat has been grown for hundreds of years, and like many other agricultural commodities, it has had impacts on the environment around it. These impacts include salinity, soil erosion and degradation, water pollution, and threats to natural **habitats**.

Salinity

When land is cleared to plant large areas of wheat, the landscape and its **ecosystems** change. The removal of vegetation causes the water beneath the ground to rise up because there are no plants to absorb it. Salt, which is found naturally in the ground, is dissolved by the rising water and brought to the surface. Over time, high levels of salt build up, making it impossible to grow crops, such as wheat. This problem is known as salinity.

Soil Erosion and Degradation

When wheat is planted in the same plot of land every year, the quality of the soil slowly deteriorates. It loses nutrients and this eventually affects the quality of the wheat grown. The clearing of land for wheat farming can also lead to soil erosion, where exposed soil is blown away by the wind or washed away by water flowing over the ground. Soil erosion can have serious effects on nearby waterways.

White land is clear evidence of salinity in this wheat-growing area of Bruce Rock, Western Australia.

Water Pollution

Chemical fertilizers are commonly used in wheat farming to add nutrients to the soil. However, excess fertilizer can find its way into nearby rivers and streams, as a result of soil erosion. Chemicals in the fertilizer can lead to the growth of **algal blooms** in the water. When the water is covered by an algal bloom, sunlight is prevented from reaching **aquatic** plants and animals. Deprived of sunlight, these plants and animals will die. Entire ecosystems may be affected by this.

Chemical fertilisers used on these wheat fields, located by a river, may be washed into the water.

Threats to Natural Habitats

The commercial farming of wheat requires large areas of land. As populations grow and more wheat is needed, the amount of land needed to grow wheat will also increase. This means more land will be cleared, and more plants and animals will lose their natural habitats. It may become very important in the future to find ways of producing wheat without endangering the lives and habitats of living things in wheat-growing areas.

"After close to 200 years of farming in some areas and as little as 30 years in others, we are seeing a lot of warning signs that all is not well with the soil and water that underpin our agricultural success ... farmers won't be able to keep up production if the quality of soil keeps declining."

Dr Anna Ridley, scientist
(Source: www.abc.net.au/landline/stories/s116302.htm)

Social Issues and Wheat

In many **developing countries**, agriculture is the most important sector of the economy. It is common for a large portion of the population to be involved in farming. Although they do not get paid very much, very few of these farmers have any other options. They must accept the low prices they are paid and continue farming their crops.

Poverty and Farming

There is a great deal of poverty in parts of Africa, Asia, and Latin America, where struggling farmers tend to small wheat crops. Often, poor soil, lack of water, crop diseases, and pests limit their productivity and force them to use chemical fertilizers, which can damage the environment. What little wheat they produce usually attracts a very low price. They are trapped in a cycle of poverty that few can break out of.

In some developing countries, wheat is still sown by hand because growers cannot afford advanced machinery to do the job for them.

The International Maize and Wheat Improvement Center

The International Maize and Wheat Improvement Center (known as CIMMYT, the initials of its original Spanish name) is a nonprofit organization that helps wheat farmers in more than 100 developing countries break out of poverty. It aims to achieve this by helping farmers implement **sustainable** and productive farming strategies. In doing so, the farmers are transformed from **subsistence** farmers to commercial farmers, producing enough wheat to both feed their families and earn a profit from their crops.

The CIMMYT in Bangladesh

Bangladesh is a densely populated country in South Asia, where most farmers live in poverty and lead a subsistence lifestyle. They struggle to grow enough wheat to feed their families, let alone to sell. Most wheat farmers only have small plots of land on which to grow their crops. The CIMMYT has provided many Bangladeshi wheat farmers with a machine called a power tiller-operated seeder. This machine allows farmers to prepare the soil in less time and to plant larger areas using fewer workers. The machine also plants seeds to the correct depth, resulting in more seeds germinating and yields increasing. By 2008, more than 25,000 Bangladeshi wheat farmers had benefited from access to power tiller-operated seeders.

In Bangladesh, the CIMMYT is helping wheat growers shift from subsistence wheat-farming to commercial wheat-farming.

MORE ABOUT...
The Work of the CIMMYT

The CIMMYT's Global Wheat Program aims to improve food security for poor people living in parts of Africa, Asia, and Latin America, where wheat-growing areas suffer from poor rainfall, poor soil, crop diseases, and extremes of temperature.

25

Is the Wheat Industry Sustainable?

To sustain something is to keep it going for a very long time. There are three aspects to keeping the wheat industry sustainable: protecting the environment in which wheat is grown, making sure wheat-growing communities can survive, and maintaining the demand for wheat.

Reducing the Environmental Impact of Wheat Farming

Some of the key environmental issues for wheat farming are salinity, soil erosion and degradation, and water pollution. If wheat farming is to become environmentally sustainable, solutions to these problems are needed.

- New water management systems for wheat growers may help fight salinity. Planting **native** trees and other vegetation in wheat belts will also help reduce salinity.

- New agricultural technology can help prevent soil erosion by planting seeds without disturbing the surrounding soil. **Crop rotation** can help prevent soil degradation. Certain crops, such as alfalfa, can replace many of the nutrients that wheat has removed from the soil. The soil will become fertile again and will be ready to grow wheat once more.

- Crop rotation may also help reduce the need for chemical fertilizers. This means less fertilizer will get washed into waterways.

A disease called stem rust has affected these wheat stalks. Stem rust can devastate entire crops.

Threats to Wheat Growers

Wheat growers rely on good yields to earn a living. Unfortunately, nature sometimes gets in the way of this. Droughts, floods, and frosts can damage wheat crops or even destroy them. Plant diseases and pests can also have a devastating impact on crops. Several crop failures in a row could put a grower under severe financial pressure.

Government assistance, such as drought or flood relief, may be made available to wheat growers to help them through difficult times. They may also benefit from the development of wheat varieties that can better resist climate events, diseases, and pests.

Scientists are developing new varieties of wheat that are more resistant to disease and require less water and fertilizer.

Maintaining the demand for wheat

As wheat is used to make many staple foods, demand for this commodity will remain strong and is likely to rise as the world's population grows. The challenge is to ensure an ongoing supply of wheat. Research and development may provide growers with new strains of wheat that can withstand climate events. This may ensure that wheat crops endure long droughts or severe frosts with little effect on yields. Improved farming methods may help growers find better ways to plant, grow, and harvest their wheat.

The Future of the Wheat Industry

Like many agricultural industries, the wheat industry must find a way to feed a growing world population, while caring for the environment and keeping the price of wheat at an affordable level.

Better Wheat Varieties

To ensure that there is enough wheat to feed the world in the future, researchers at CIMMYT are genetically modifying wheat varieties to make them capable of:
- withstanding drought
- resisting disease and pests
- growing in poor soil
- producing higher yields
- providing more nutritional goodness

The work done by such organizations is important to the future of the industry. Improved wheat varieties will ensure that one of the world's most important crops does not run out and will survive **climate change**.

Genetically-modified wheat is a controversial development. New varieties may have higher yields and be more resistant to drought and disease, but are they safe?

Genetically Modified Wheat

Some wheat varieties may be developed in laboratories to produce significantly higher yields or to resist drought or disease. However, many consumers have expressed concerns that the effects of genetically modified foods on human health are not fully known yet. They also fear that something as small as pollen from genetically modified wheat could contaminate regular wheat if both varieties are stored near each other.

Improving Farming Techniques

There is a strong likelihood that more farms in the future will grow several different **cash crops** each year and rear livestock. This is called mixed farming. It provides different sources of income if one crop fails to yield a good harvest. Growing different cash crops is also an effective form of crop rotation.

Research Will Show the Way

Climate change is having an impact on the way we grow our food. Severe frosts and prolonged droughts have destroyed precious wheat crops. The wheat varieties and farming methods we have relied on up to this point may no longer be effective, if the climate continues to change.

Research and development is needed to prepare the wheat industry for an uncertain future. This is likely to take time and will cost a lot of money. However, the benefits will be clear when farmers are able to grow crops that provide good yields, even in years of poor rainfall or cold snaps.

Regardless of how the world changes, it is certain that in the future there will be more mouths to feed. A healthy wheat industry will ensure that there is enough food for everyone.

New developments in the wheat industry include a sensor that helps determine the right amount of fertilizer to add to a growing crop and the best time to add it.

Find Out More

Web Sites for Further Information

- ## The health benefits of wheat
Learn more about the healthy properties of whole-wheat foods.
www.whfoods.com/genpage.php?tname=foodspice&dbid=66

- ## The different types of wheat flours
Learn more about varieties of wheat flour.
www.wheatfoods.org/AboutWheat-wheat-flours/Index.htm

- ## How to bake bread
Learn more about baking bread in the traditional way.
www.instructables.com/id/How-To-Make-Bread-without-a-bread-machine/

- ## Wheat trading defined and explained
Learn more about how wheat is traded.
www.tradertech.com/information/wheattrading.asp

Focus Questions

These questions might help you think about some of the issues raised in this book.

- Why are scientists trying to develop new and improved strains of wheat?

- What are the main arguments for and against genetically-modified wheat?

- Should genetically-modified wheat be introduced on a large scale?

- Is wheat the most important food product?

Glossary

agricultural	related to farming or used for farming
algal blooms	slimy growths of algae on the surface of water
aquatic	living or growing in water
cash crops	crops grown by farmers to be sold for money rather than for their own use
climate change	a change in the world's weather conditions over a period of time, due to natural events or human activities
crop rotation	a farming method where different crops are grown in the same field at different times, in order to nourish the soil and prevent crop disease
demand	the amount of a product consumers want to buy
developing countries	countries in the early stages of becoming industrialized
domestic	relating to a person's own country
economy	a system that organizes the production, distribution, and exchange of goods and services, as well as incomes
ecosystems	communities of plants and animals that interact with one another and with the environments in which they live
European Union	an association of 27 European countries set up in 1993, with its own currency and market
export	a product which is sold to another country; or the action of sending a product to another country to sell it
germinate	to develop into a plant
habitats	the natural environments of animals or plants
hybrid	having the best characteristics of two different types of plant
imports	products which are bought or brought in from another country; or the action of buying and bringing a product into a country
mature	complete their natural growth
native	growing naturally in an area
natural resources	the naturally occurring, useful wealth of a region or country, such as land, forests, coal, oil, gas, and water
pollen	a powder produced by the male part of a flower, which causes the female part of the same flower to produce seeds
quotas	limits on the amount of certain commodities which can be imported
stockpiling	storing a large amount of something for use in the future
subsidies	money or other contributions given by the government to help someone or an organization reduce their business costs
subsistence	having just enough food and other essentials to survive, but no more
supply	the amount of a product that producers are able to sell
surplus	an amount which is more than is needed
sustainable	developed or designed so that the production of a commodity can continue for a long time
yield	to produce; or the amount that is produced

Index